acknowledgements · This package is the result of a great deal of giving and care by many people. I would like to thank them all very specially, in particular those who gave of their artistic talents. My thanks also to Gary Marshfield for ideas and feedback on the content of the package, and to Margaret Wellings for typing the manuscript.

My particular thanks to Pat Schleger and Virginia Foden for designing this book and taking such personal interest in its production.

A special thank you to Mary Emmerson Law and the staff at Churchill Livingstone involved in this collaborative venture.

pages 28, 72, 76, 91 · Grateful acknowledgement to Mel Calman for the use of his drawings © Mel Calman 1970

pages vi, 5, 8, 42, 54, 55, 56 · photos by kind permission of Stefan Buzas

page xi · photo by permission of Alan Murgatroyd

pages 7, 24, 50, 93 · photos by kind permission of Robin Hart

page 39 · photo by kind permission of Suzanne Sziranyi

page 40 · photo by Kenneth Sinclair

page 48 · photo by Hans Schleger

pages 9, 13, 18, 27, 41, 63, 80, 94, 104 · cartoons by kind permission of Richard Smith

pages 30–37 · text and drawings of exercises by Catherine Robinson

page 14 · drawing by Picasso by permission of Verve Publications, Paris, from 'Suite de 180 dessins de Picasso' 1954

page 17 · clay figures from Turfan, China (Tan Dynasty) by kind permission of the Cultural Attaché of the People's Republic of China, London

page 65 · from a painting by Hans Schleger 1939

page 70 · lithograph by kind permission of Leo Baeck Institute, New York, and the editor of the Year Book of the Leo Baeck Institute, London Dr Arnold Paucker

page 97 · photo by Fulvio Roiter, by permission of L'Oeil Revue d'Art, Paris 1974 no. 228–229, p9

page 100 · photo by A Feininger in 'Das Antlitz der Natur' 1957. By permission of Doermersche Verlagsanstalt Munich

pages 98, 99 · symbols from Koch R (1955) The Book of Signs, New York, Dover Publications Inc.

page 108 · photo from Bancroft J D and Stevens A (1977) Theory and Practice of Histological Techniques, p245 by kind permission of Churchill Livingstone, Edinburgh

pages ix, 19, 38, 58, 79, 85 · workshop pictures by kind permission of the people who took part in various workshops

book design and diagrams · Hans Schleger and Associates

Contents

beginning with
Awareness

a learners' handbook

Verena Tschudin BSc(Hons) RGN RM Dip Counselling

Churchill Livingstone
Edinburgh London Melbourne and New York 1991

CHURCHILL LIVINGSTONE
Medical Division of Longman Group UK Limited

Distributed in the United States of America by Churchill Livingstone Inc.
1560 Broadway, New York, N.Y. 10036, and by associated companies,
branches and representatives throughout the world.

First published 1991

ISBN 0-443-04292-6

British Library Cataloguing in Publication Data
Tschudin, Verena
  Beginning with awareness: a learner's handbook.
  1. Man. Perception
  I. Title
  153.7

Produced by Longman Singapore Publishers Pte Ltd
Printed in Singapore

Self-awareness

Why should you want to learn self-awareness?

You may have many reasons. Or you may not have thought about this precisely and cannot answer that question now.

We are all aware, and often acutely so. But we are often not aware of things and people and ourselves at the right time and in the correct way. Hindsight can then be a painful teacher. Self-awareness is not an end in itself. If it becomes that, it is egoism. Learning self-awareness is for personal and professional growth. It is for better and more adequate functioning as a person in relation to other persons.

Self-awareness – or greater and more accurate awareness – gives you the possibility to make sense of events and relationships. It gives you the ability to experience something fully and not be taken over by it. It gives you the skill to be involved but not over-involved; to give yourself and to know when to withdraw; to be yourself and to let others be themselves; to act and to take charge and know when you are acted upon and taken charge of. Self-awareness gives you integrity: not licence to do as you please, but freedom to choose and act in the best way for yourself and others.

How do you learn self-awareness? Neither this book – nor any other book will *give* you awareness. But through exercises alone and with others you will, it is hoped, learn to listen to yourself, to who you are, what you are, and how you are.

Self-awareness goes on all the time. Greater awareness leads to greater change.

The outer world influences the inner world, and through the inner world we influence our surroundings. The vehicle for that is the body.

Therefore all these areas have to be looked at if we want to become more aware. To do so in a sequence is somewhat artificial. You may therefore like to go from one section of the book to another, to follow the flow of your awareness. When you do that, simply be aware that that is indeed what you are doing.

There is no *theory* as such in the book, for awareness is not about knowledge, but about being; it is not about answers, but about experience, and discovery. The theory in this book is the one which you give it, and in the workshop receive from your colleagues.

Nevertheless, I have included explanations, elaborations, and highlights on certain points. There are also snippets from various sources dotted about. These are all texts and thoughts which I have found helpful. But they may not speak to you in the same way. I invite you therefore, as part of this work of self-awareness, to find your own texts, phrases, vignettes and sayings, and either write them into the book, or in a diary. They may be illuminating to you in the future, both for yourself and for use in the workshop.

The exercises in the workshop will be group-oriented. Some of them ask for paintings and drawings to express awareness. In this handbook you will find a number of drawings made at such workshops by different people. (Their reproduction here loses some of the impact of the colours in which they were made.) You may like to make your own drawings and paintings while you work through the handbook.

This book should be given to you as a preparation for a workshop on awareness. The workshop should deepen and clarify any learning made. But this book does also stand on its own. Your learning by yourself is also valid.

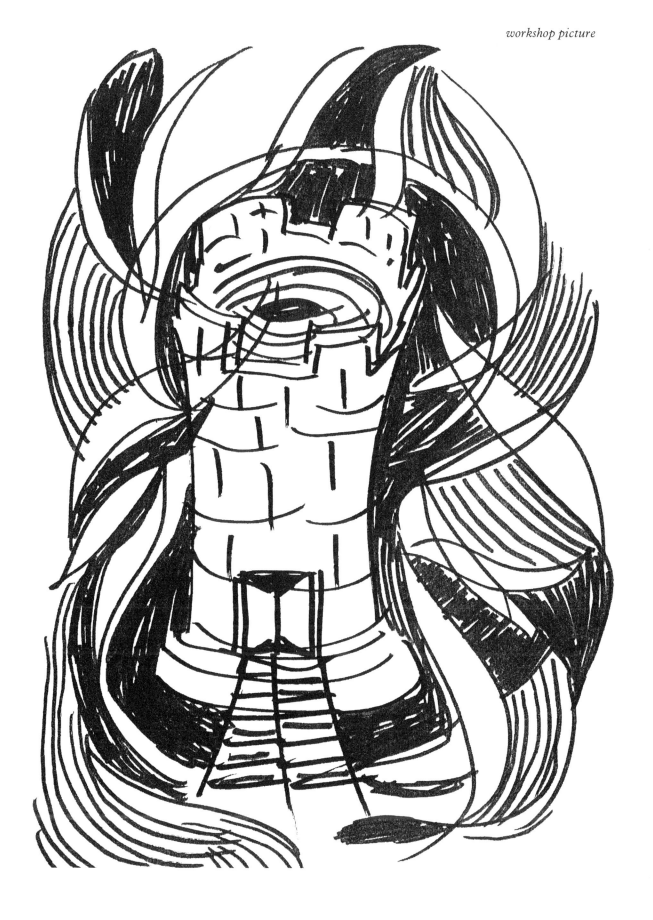

'Egocentricity is morbid preoccupation with self and opaqueness to the needs of the other. But there is nothing egocentric about caring for myself.'

Mayeroff, 1972

'Skilled helpers have their own human problems, from which they do not retreat. They explore their own behaviour and know who they are. They know what it means to be helped and have a deep respect for the helping process and its power for better or for worse. Even though they are living effectively, they also know they are in process, that each stage of life has its own developmental tasks and crises.'

Egan, 1986

Self-awareness is a process which leads to greater wholeness

for professional growth and development

integrity

meaning in life

assertiveness

self-awareness

honesty with self and others

job satisfaction

personal growth and development

good career choices

'Wait – cognize – will what is willed – dare.'

Anon

'Gathered together in common vulnerability, we discover how much we have to give to each other.'

Nouwen, 1982

'The way he says I – what he means when he says I – decides where a man belongs and where he goes. The word "I" is the true shibboleth of humanity.
Listen to it.'

Buber, 1937

The outer world

the go-between world of the body & the senses

the inside world

integrity

The outer world

Look through this book and make any notes you like.

Read the exercises which are marked by numbers in the black boxes and do them, as much as you are able to, particularly on the pages marked *Skills Sheet* where space is provided.

If thoughts and feelings emerge for you which are not mentioned here, do note them down anywhere – they may be important for you.

Room

Please sit down somewhere comfortable.

When you are settled, look all round the room.

Look at the room as if you were seeing it for the first time.

Notice any interesting features. Look at them and become aware of them.

Take your time and look at any object as long as it makes sense.

Object

When you have seen as many objects as you want to, let your eyes rest on one which draws your attention.

Be aware of the attraction it has for you. Go to it and handle it. Feel it. Touch it. Let it make an impression on you.

Hold the object as if you had never seen anything like it. Turn it over. Notice how it is made and put together. Be aware of its weight, its smell, its beauty. Hold it and feel it as long as you like.

If you can be aware of the **being** of this object be aware of . . .

the woodness of wood

the colourfulness of colour

the paperness of paper

the plant-life of a plant

the clearness of glass

View

Now walk to the window and look out quite deliberately.

Be aware of the day or night.

Be aware of the weather.

Simply notice what you see.

As you notice each thing, acknowledge it by saying silently or aloud . . .

I see the blue sky

I see a white house

I see a car going by

When you next go to work, give yourself the time and opportunity to look at the building afresh.

Notice the house: the bricks or stones, the windows.

Notice the door in particular, and walk through it deliberately.

Notice any smells, and special attractions, any broken bits, marks and chipped areas, any litter or particular features.

Don't interpret anything, but simply be aware of them and of yourself in relation to them.

Rub your fingers over any points which are significant. Do this as attentively as you can and let their **being** become alive to you.

Influences

The outside world of things and objects influences us all the time, if we like it or not.

Make a list of the things which you like to influence you from that world. Be as specific as you can in naming the objects.

Now list the things which you don't like but which influence you nevertheless. Be specific.

Among the things may be . . .

the weather

houses

rivers, bridges

trains

locations

Events

Today .... a feather came to rest on my shoe

I received a letter with unexpectedly good news

a bird was singing just above me as I walked by

a child at the bus-stop smiled at me

I found a 10p piece in the street

a neighbour put a hyacinth in the hall
and the whole house is full of scent

'Those undeserved joys
which come uncalled
and make us more pleased
than grateful
are they that sing.'

Henry David Thoreau

Have you had any undeserved joys today?

Media

Think for a moment how the media influences you.

Television

Radio

Newspapers

Advertisements

Books

Posters

Announcements

Be aware of how these are influencing you today.

Be aware how any **one** of them has influenced you. Have you welcomed it (e.g. you bought the book) or was it simply there (e.g. a radio in a shop)?

Leisure

You will have had some leisure today. Think of some things from the outer world connected with leisure which influenced you. What was important about that?

'All intellectual improvement arises from leisure.'

Samuel Johnson

4-1.54.

Art

Remember the last time you had contact with art

paintings

sculpture

music

theatre

dance

What memory stands out for you from that contact?

How does art influence you?

If you were on a desert island, what art would you find there?
What would be different for you between that and what is generally known as art?

Space

Try to be aware of the space around you

your living space: how many square feet do you have?

at work: how close do you sit to your neighbour?

when you travel: how much distance do you leave between the car in front and yours?

in a crowded train: how long is it before you become anxious or claustrophobic?

As you go through the day, be aware of the occasions and moments when you have a lot of space – little space – invade someone's space – have your space invaded. Be aware of the space around you, and also of the feelings which this creates in you. Do not analyse your feelings, simply be *aware* of them.

Routine

Much of life is routine.

What sort of things, would you say, are routine in your life? Let yourself be surprised by the things which you call routine.

make a list of them . . .

. . . .

. . . .

. . . .

. . . .

. . . .

Time

'With thee conversing I forget all time' *Milton*

- If you can, take an alarm clock, or any clock or watch that ticks.

- Sit very still and listen to the ticks for 3 minutes. Simply concentrate on the ticks, and on the fact of time.

- Be aware of the length – the time – of 3 minutes.

- Think back over the past and remember the longest 3 minutes which you lived through.

- Try to remember the shortest 3 days in your life.

- What made these events so long or so short? Call to memory the feelings and reasons for your awareness of time.

Other people

People influence us more than anything else which surrounds us; and we influence others.

Make a list of the people who influence you most.

. . . .

. . . .

. . . .

. . . .

. . . .

. . . .

. . . .

. . . .

. . . .

Now number them from 1–10 in the order in which they influence you. This influence may be happy or unhappy. Simply be aware of the **amount** of influence.

Now think of the people whom you influence.

Pick out three names from that list and write against them in what way *you* influence them.

This kind of awareness may be like taking a step back. The pressures of life demand that we get on, move up, acquire things to help us forward.

Noticing something for itself is therefore like standing still. To hold something and feel its intrinsic worth is essentially a lonely business. *Time stands still.*

It seems necessary that occasionally we do this. Always being on the move for more and better things means that we tend to walk by the essentials; we lose the capacity to celebrate (things, events, ourselves). To stand still, to notice, to be aware, is necessary in order to go forward more fully, more adequately.

There may be other areas, things, objects, or events in the outer world which are important to you, or influence you, but are not mentioned here. Would you like to make a note of them for your own interest, or learning, memory or awareness?

Body awareness

'I know I have the body
of a weak and feeble woman,
but I have the heart
and stomach of a king.'

Queen Elizabeth I

We experience something on the outside, but we know it on the inside. The body and the senses are the vehicle for experiencing – handling – the outer world and for perceiving – understanding – in the inner world.

Our language is full of expressions using body-parts to point to something deeper

experiencing a gut reaction

having two left feet

putting your foot in it

a warm-hearted person

light-fingered

being two-faced

add your own . . .

. . . .

. . . .

. . . .

. . . .

Your body

Relax for a moment and become *aware* of your body.

Become aware of the things which are not functioning well in your body

pain – locate it

headache

pre-menstrual tension

dry skin

add your own . . .

. . . .

. . . .

. . . .

. . . .

. . . .

Which of these are you attending to? Which do you neglect?

Be *aware* of the choices you make in your attention, but do not judge them.

Now relax a little more deeply.

There are nine different systems in your body

skeletal

muscular

circulatory

respiratory

digestive

urinary

endocrine

reproductive

nervous

Slowly imagine how each of these systems now works for you. Be *aware* of how these systems function. Stay with each system for as long as you can.

Make a mental note, or a list, of any thoughts which come to you as you do this exercise.

I've got a HEADACHE all over my BODY...

As a further exercise try to become *aware* of any particular part or system of your body which functions well.

We tend to take our body and health for granted and only notice anything which goes wrong.

Give your body a treat and positively enjoy what is going well. Be *aware* of as many things as you can, and perhaps write them down.

How to approach these exercises

Do not hurry. Don't feel you have to do all the sequences at one time. You will get more benefit from doing a few movements slowly, and with attention, than rushing through the whole programme. If you wish to do all three sequences, do them in the order shown.

Breathing should be gentle and slow. Try to feel that the movement of breath starts in the abdomen, and then moves up into the chest. This develops deep diaphragmatic breathing which helps to relieve tension. The best way to practise this is to lie on the back with the knees bent, and the feet and knees slightly apart. (Read the instructions for the first posture in Sequence 3.) If you rest the hands on the lower abdomen it is easier to focus on the movement of the breath. Once you have established the abdominal breathing, then allow the breath to flow deeper so that you feel the sideways expansion of the ribs. Be particularly attentive to the outbreath, noticing how the ribcage relaxes back, and then the abdomen sinks down gently at the end of the breath.

As you become more familiar with the exercises, try to co-ordinate the movements with the breathing, as explained in the instructions. Re-read the notes from time to time, to make sure you are practising correctly. Some of the instructions are specifically there to guide you into approaching the exercises safely.

When to do the exercises

You may find it helpful to do a few stretches when you first get up in the morning. If you have only a few minutes, do Sequence 1. The other two sequences are particularly useful for easing out aching backs after a day's work, though they will also help to give flexibility and strength to your back before you start your day. Allow yourself time and quiet to practise. Even if you have only a few minutes for yourself, remember that it is *your* space, and a time to become still and centred. You will then feel better prepared to meet the demands that others make on you.

Avoid practising immediately after a meal. Don't do the exercises in a stuffy or smoky room. Your body needs good fresh air. Ideally you should find a quiet place where you won't be interrupted, but this is often impossible. If you focus on the gentle inflow and outflow of breath as you practise, it will enable you to keep attentive to the movements, and help you to overcome distractions. Beware of becoming resentful of people around you who seem to be invading your quiet space. See if you can find the inner stillness which is there with you whenever you return to the gentle rhythm of your breath.

Finally, treat your body gently. Do not overstretch or set yourself impossible goals, and never force a position if it is painful. The aim of these exercises is to help to bring your body back to a healthy balance, not to pull it apart. If you have back problems read the captions carefully and don't take any risks. Take responsibility for your own body, and respect its limitations, and remember to relax for a few moments after each sequence.

There is a vital interrelationship between the mind and the body, and the link between them is the breath. Keep attentive to your breathing as you practise, and you will be helping to restore a sense of balance and harmony within yourself.

1 Stand with the feet slightly apart. Stand tall and relaxed, breathing gently. Relax the shoulders, the hands and the tummy. Lengthen the back of the neck, directing the top of the head towards the ceiling. Ease out the lower back by releasing the knees slightly, and relaxing the pelvis, allowing the coccyx to hang down. The pelvis should not be tilted either backwards or forwards. This position is known as 'Mountain' pose, and represents stillness, stability and centredness. Return to 'Mountain' after each stretch, breathing gently, and giving time for the muscles to relax.

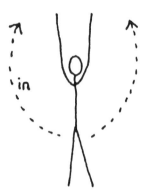

2 Full stretch: breathe in, raise the arms, coming up onto the toes, and stretch through the body. Breathe out and relax.

3 Repeat, stretching through the right side, and then the left.

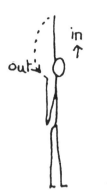

4 Breathe in, raise the right arm above the head, and bend the left arm behind the back, with the hand between the shoulder blades. Breathe out and drop the right hand behind the head, and if possible, link the fingers. If your hands don't meet, start again, easing the left elbow into position with the right hand, before raising the right arm. You may well find that your fingers are still a long way apart. If so, try again, holding a scarf or handkerchief in the upper hand, and catch hold of it with the lower hand. Gradually work your hands towards each other. With practice the gap will gradually get smaller. Repeat, with the left arm above the head. You may notice that one side is easier than the other. Release and relax the shoulders, elbows, wrists and fingers.

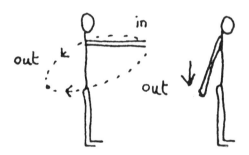

5 Breathe in, bringing the arms straight out in front. Breathe out, bringing the hands behind the back and linking the fingers. Gently pull backwards and downwards, pulling the shoulder blades together. Breathe in and release, breathe out and relax.

6 Breathe in, raising arms above the head. Take the right wrist in the left hand, and pull the arms gently backwards, breathing out. Feel the stretch between the shoulder blades. Breathe in and release, breathe out and relax the arms to the sides. Repeat with the left wrist.

7 Rotate the shoulders up towards the ears and down, first backwards, then forwards, breathing gently.

8 Slightly bend the knees. This will reduce strain on the backs of the legs and lower back. Breathing out, slowly let the upper body hang forward from the waist, by dropping the chin towards the chest, and letting the spine roll gently forwards. Let the arms hang loose, and the head relax down. Breathe gently, allowing the body to let go a little more with each outbreath. Breathing in, slowly unwind from the base of the spine, bringing the head up last. If you feel pain in your back, or know you have any weakness in your back, approach this cautiously, or leave it out.

9 Repeat 'Mountain' pose.

 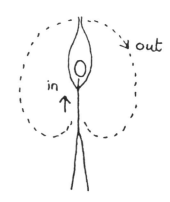

10 'Swimming in space' breath: bring hands together in a prayer position in front of the chest. Breathe in, raising the arms above the head, palms together. Breathe out, bringing the arms down and round in a wide circle, palms down, and return to prayer position. Repeat slowly for as long as you wish, keeping the eyes closed, and letting the breath flow deeply and rhythmically.

11 Return to 'Mountain' pose, breathing gently. Follow the outbreath. Relax as you breathe out, feeling your weight sinking down into your feet. Allow yourself to be completely supported by the ground beneath you.

Sequence 2 / developing strength and flexibility in the back

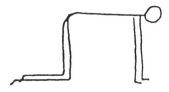

1 Kneel with the hands, knees and feet slightly apart, with the tops of the feet resting on the floor, and the palms down. (If this position leads to uncomfortable strain on the wrists, the weight may be supported on the fists.) The spine should be straight, and the neck in line with the spine. Relax the tummy, and breathe gently. Return to this position after stretches 3, 4, 5 and 6.

2 Breathe in. Breathe out and raise the head up and drop the small of the back down.

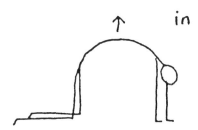

3 Breathe in, drop the head down, and arch the back up as far as you can. Repeat 2 and 3 slowly. Return to position 1.

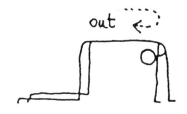

4 Breathe in. Breathe out, turning the head over the right shoulder, looking towards the left heel. Breathe in as you return to 1. Repeat to the left.

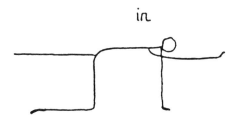

5 Breathe in, raising the *right* arm and the *left* leg, and stretch. Breathe out and relax. Repeat with the *left* arm and the *right* leg.

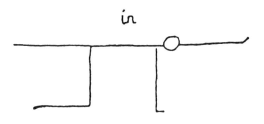

6 Breathe in, raising the *right* arm and the *right* leg, and stretch. Breathe out and relax. Repeat to the left. These two movements help to develop your balance and co-ordination.

out

7 Sit back on the heels. Breathe in. Breathe out, sliding the hands forwards with the arms comfortably apart, and bring the forehead to the floor. Stretch the arms.

out

8 From this position, slowly bring the hands back alongside the feet, with the backs of the hands on the floor. Relax the shoulders, close the eyes, and breathe gently. Let go as you breathe out. Remain in your final position as long as you feel relaxed, and then slowly sit up, breathing in. If you find this position uncomfortable, or you find difficulty in breathing, try putting a cushion underneath the head, lie on the side curled up, or proceed to the first position in Sequence 3.

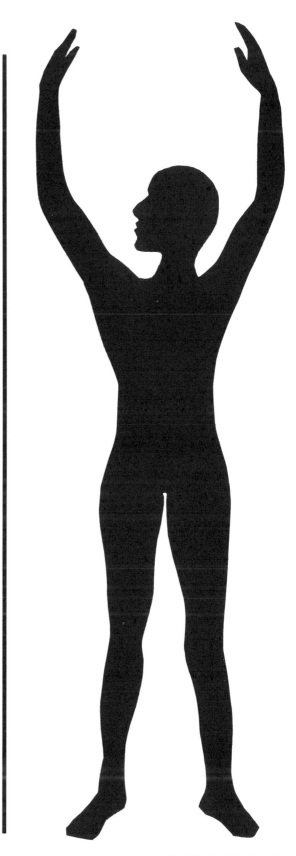

Sequence 3 / relaxation: easing out the lower back

1 Lie on the floor, on a blanket or carpet, in a warm place away from draughts. Bend the knees, and place the soles of the feet on the floor, with the feet and knees slightly apart, and the head in line with the body. The arms should be a little way from the body. Turn the palms upwards, and relax the hands. If you feel strain in the neck, place a couple of books under the head, to raise it slightly. Breathe gently, feeling the movement of breath in the abdomen. As you breathe in, feel the tummy pushing upwards. As you breathe out, let the tummy relax back towards the spine.

Notice in this position that the small of the back can relax closer to the floor than when the legs are extended. This is the best relaxation position to adopt if you have pain or stiffness in your lower back.

2 Let the legs slide down to the floor one at a time, lying slightly apart, and let the feet fall outwards. Continue to breathe gently and relax.

in

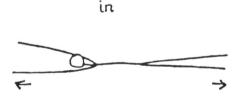

3 Full stretch: Breathe in, raising the arms behind the head, and stretch through the whole body. Breathe out and release, keeping the arms above the head.

in

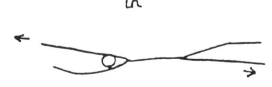

4 Breathe in, stretching the *right* arm and the *left* leg, keeping the opposite arm and leg completely relaxed. Breathe out, and release the stretch. Repeat with the *left* arm and the *right* leg.

in

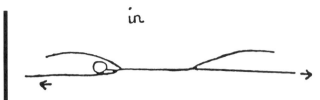

5 Breathe in, stretching the *right* arm and the *right* leg, keeping the left side completely relaxed. Breathe out, and release the stretch. Repeat to the left, and return to position 2.

6 Breathe in. Breathe out, bending the knees towards the chest. Link the hands over the knees, and gently rock from side to side. Rest in the centre.

7 Place the hands on top of the knees. Breathe in, pushing the knees away from the chest, keeping the big toes touching. Breathe out, letting the knees come apart, and circle round back to the chest, feeling the widest possible rotation in the hip joint. Repeat three times.

8 Change the direction of the circles. Start with the knees close to the chest. Breathe in, letting them come apart, and circle round till the knees come together. Breathe out, drawing the closed knees in towards the chest. Repeat three times.

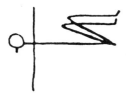

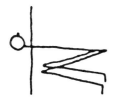

9 Keeping the knees close to the chest, breathe in. Breathe out, extending the arms out to the sides, with the backs of the hands on the floor. With the knees together, breathe in. Breathe out, lowering the knees gently sideways towards the floor to the right, and turn the head to the left. *Do not* force the knees down. If it is too much stretch for your back, come up slowly. Breathe in as you bring the knees up. Repeat, lowering the knees to the left, and turning the head to the right.

10 Link the fingers together over the knees. Breathe in. Breathe out, bringing the head gently up towards the knees. Do not force this position. Breathe out, relaxing the head back, and releasing the knees.

11 Relax with the knees bent, the feet on the floor, and the feet and knees slightly apart. Position 1.

12 Either remain in this position, if you are more comfortable, or extend the legs to the floor, in position 2. Close the eyes and breathe gently. Feel the body becoming heavy, and sinking into the floor as you breathe out, and completely relax. Remain in your final relaxation position for as long as possible.

These exercises draw on elements from both Yoga and T'ai Chi, and have been designed to be of particular help to nurses. They focus on the importance of maintaining a strong, flexible back, for people used to heavy lifting and long hours of standing. They help to relieve tension and stress in the neck and shoulders, which so often leads to headaches or muscular strain; and they show ways to relax and let go after a hard day's work. As the body learns to relax deeply, so does the mind, gradually developing a sense of inner stillness, equilibrium and harmony.

Clothes

Now become *aware* of what you are wearing.

Start with your shoes.
As you work up from the feet, be aware of each item
which you wear.
Notice what the garment is, and notice its colour and
texture.

As you become aware of your clothing, you might
find that with it you are giving a message to the
world.

Be aware of this message (don't interpret it) and
perhaps write it down here as a record.

Become, or be, *aware* of how you are sitting or standing. Notice your posture.

Notice how your hands, your legs, are.

Notice how you are holding your head.

What expression do you have on your face?

Be aware of what other people are wearing, or the postures they take.

Be aware of the judgements you make about them. Simply take note of these judgements. You learn more about yourself by noticing the judgements you make than by interpreting them.

You might like to sit yourself in front of a mirror. Look at the person in front of you.

Take all sorts of positions   relaxed, tense, legs crossed, uncrossed, head to one side, or straight, being friendly, or pre-occupied.

As you see each of these positions, notice what they do for you. Notice how you feel in that position.

Notice what you feel as the **recipient** of each position, as the person who watches you.

You might like to note which position you like best
to be in
to be seen to be in.

Make a note of which position affirms you most
as the giver
as the receiver.

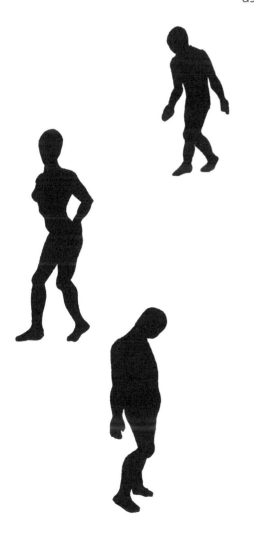

Awareness of the senses

I **smell** the freshly baked bread as I approach the bakery

I **see** steamy crusty loaves like my mother used to bake when I was young. I buy a loaf

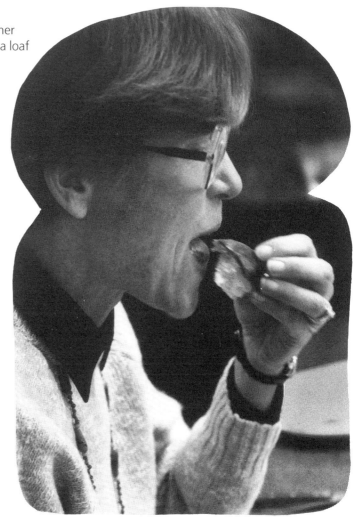

I **touch** the loaf, feeling its warmth in the palm of my hand

I **hear** the crackling of the crust as I cut the fresh bread

I **taste** the fresh bread – there is nothing like it!

bread

the outer world

the go-between world of the senses	the inner world		
seeing	hunger	my own that of others the sick the starving millions for food/companionship	
smelling	bread	satisfaction keeping alive the bread and salt of brotherhood communion	
touching	family	sharing what we have eating together memories	
hearing			
tasting	making bread	creativity feeding myself and those I love farmers harvest agricultural policies politics	

The senses

The senses open up the inner world; they make it accessible

● Love goes through the stomach

● I see what you mean

● A disagreement leaves a bad taste

● 'The touches of sweet harmony'   *Shakespeare*

● She could never hear the noise of gunfire without feeling sick

● I smell a rat

Try the following exercises, concentrating on each one of the senses.

As you do the exercises allow any thoughts, memories, images or associations to come to you and be aware of where this takes you. Perhaps make a note of anything significant which comes to your mind.

 *smell*

Breathe in gently and slowly and notice any smells or odours around you.

Notice where and how you experience a particular smell.

Stay with the smell and let any thoughts connected with smells come up in you. Make any associations you like.

As nurses we are all familiar with describing smells and odours of specimens.

What smells do you like?

Why?

Under which circumstances?

Blind people develop a strong sense of touch: for the next 24 hours be aware of your touch, and how you touch.

Rub your fingers very gently over a piece of clothing. Notice the sensation.
With your hand, rub an area of carpet vigorously. Be aware of the sensation in your fingertips.

Notice how your fingers feel, but notice also how far the sensation travels: up your arm, to the spine, to the brain.

Notice what else you feel while doing this exercise: pleasure, annoyance. How do you feel these emotions? Where are they located? What associations do they have for you?

When you next touch a person be aware of how you do it. Be aware of the feelings inside you as you do so.

Be aware of your feelings when someone touches you.

What do you mean when you say that you are touched by something?

Take something savoury to eat (bread, crisps, lettuce). Slowly chew this and notice what you taste, and where. What is the specific sensation of taste?

Take something sweet and eat it (biscuit, chocolate). Notice the anticipation of eating this. Chew it slowly and notice how you eat it, what you sense and taste.

Then slowly swallow this food in your *awareness* down the gullet, into the stomach, and through the digestive system.

Hold your attention as long as you can, and follow where the attention goes.
Be aware of how long the taste stays.

hearing

Sit very quietly and begin to listen to all the noises around you.

Listen to any one sound in particular. Try to identify with that sound. What is that sound conveying to you?

Listen to your body and its sounds. Can you hear your heart beat? What sounds are you aware of?

make a note of the sounds you hear . . .

Look at the photograph of the **loaf of bread**. Look at it as a whole. Now look at only one detail.

What do you notice? What is the difference between the whole and the detail?

Be aware of any feelings which this stirs in you, or any memories, daydreams or moods this creates.

The senses are essential to life. Without the senses we could be in constant physical danger. You might like to make a note of the dangers which you foresee for yourself and for someone else.

Which sense would you least like to be without?

What do you **think** it would do to you to be without that sense?

Stay with that **thought** for a moment and **imagine** what it would do to you. What **feelings** might you also have if you lost that sense?

SENSITIVITY   sensuality   sensibility

sensuous   SENSE

SENSITIVE

SENSUAL

SENSATION

sensible

....
....
....
....
....
....
....
....
....
....

The senses go between physical experience and moral judgement, between the outside world and the inside world.

If you have access to a thesaurus or encyclopaedia, it may be interesting to look up these (and other relevant) words for their context and meaning.

Sexuality is a powerful and motivating force in life. *Like the senses*, it is something physical which affects us emotionally, internally. More than the senses, it is a life-force: it ensures the survival of the human race.

Some people say that sexuality is a drive, like hunger or thirst. Is this your experience?

You might like to think of some ways in which you express your sexuality every day

touching someone

dressing provocatively

make-up, perfumes, scents

posture

add your own . . .

. . . .

. . . .

. . . .

Think of some of the things which make you particularly aware of your sexuality.

It is sometimes alleged that nurses have no sexual feelings because of their constant contact with patients' bodies. Do you believe this? Is it your experience?

Do you talk with patients about sexuality?

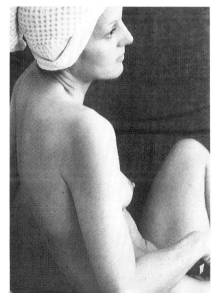

Do you talk with your friends about sexual matters and/or your sexual experiences?

How do you react to people who express their sexuality differently from yours

heterosexuals . . . .

homosexuals . . . .

bisexuals . . . .

transvestites . . . .

What does this say to you about your own sexuality?

Are you satisfied with the way in which you express your sexuality?

'Only because I understand and respond to my own needs to grow can I understand his striving to grow; I can understand in another only what I can understand in myself.'

Mayeroff, 1972

'You know me through and through, from having watched my bones take shape when I was being formed in secret, knitted together in the limbo of the womb.'

Psalm 139, 15

There will be opportunities in the workshop to discuss and reflect on any of these questions and exercises. If you would like particular help with or attention to anything, be sure to do so.

Self-awareness is a process which is learnt in contact with others. Other people's experiences and awareness will therefore help and influence you – and yours will help and influence others. Sharing, comparing and discussing are therefore very important.

workshop picture

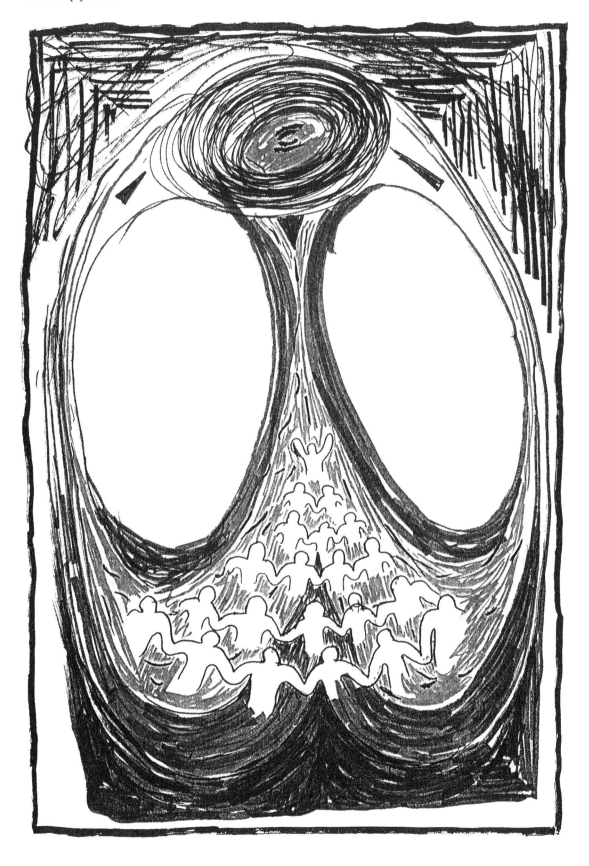

Section three   The inner world

The inner world

The inner world of thoughts and feelings is as vivid and colourful as the outside world. For some people their inner world is their *real* world; other people try to avoid it as much as possible.

The world of thoughts and feelings is a hidden world – or rather, it is a world which we can hide. No wonder it is of such interest to everyone! We would love to know what others think and feel about us: we know what we think and feel about them.

But we cannot keep the inner world hidden or hiding. The aim of any self-awareness is greater integrity through appropriate growth and development. The integrity of outer and inner, of reality and fantasy, and past, present and future in our lives is something which we constantly strive for and have to work at. As life changes, we change and with it change our ideas and interpretations.

The following exercises are pointers to awareness. They are presented out of *one* experience, and may therefore not correspond to the experience of you, the reader. Use them as and how you are able; leave those which don't speak to you now, and if you can, let those which speak to you do so fully.

'Cogito, ergo sum.'
I think, therefore I am.

As an exercise, sit quietly for 5 minutes, and notice all the thoughts which go through your mind. Be aware of your thoughts, just as they come, but don't stop them or direct them.

Were there any thoughts which were revealing?
Did you like your thoughts?
Which thoughts were helpful, which were unhelpful?
Do your thoughts constitute your being?
What would you say your thoughts are for?

You might like to repeat this exercise in a few days.
Be aware of any thoughts which recur, and if there is a pattern.
Make a note of any such patterns.

Recurring thoughts show a pattern of thinking which you might not have been aware of. This can show you a stability or maturity in thinking. It may also beg of you to change. Which do you think is more appropriate for you?

What type or level of maturity do your thoughts suggest to you?

What possible changes might your thoughts point you to?

Sit quietly and take a few slow and deep breaths.

Relax. Let the mind wander until you come to something noticeable. Take that one thought, and elaborate it. Let it go where it wants to go. Do some day-dreaming, but be aware of yourself and this thought. Notice if it goes off on a tangent, down a memory-lane, into fantasy-land; if it becomes an argument; if it deteriorates.
Do not judge the outcome, simply notice it. The learning is in the noticing, the awareness. With a judgement you do not progress.

Make a note of the thoughts which you pursued.

Take any one problem which you have at present
(e.g. to change jobs and what to do next; to produce
a piece of work; to sell the car)

Make a note of the problem . . .

Do you normally solve problems in

intuitive

consequential

strategic ways?

Tick which is closest to you.

Edward de Bono (1967) says that **intuitive** thinking
depends more on stumbling on to the right path,
than looking for it.
In **consequential** thinking we have a progression of
steps such as corrections, errors, new ideas.
Strategic thinking consists of choosing the right
steps among any number of possibilities.

We all think differently, but we can improve our less-
used thinking capacities. It is helpful to know –
or guess – how you think and how others think,
so as not to be surprised too often.

Arm... SUMMER *L'Été*

Tableau de Zéri

Value-thoughts

Look at this list of topics. Finish the sentences, preferably giving a long, explanatory ending. Add your own value-thoughts and value-statements.

Empathy is . . .

Nursing is . . .

Health is . . .

Politics is . . .

Philosophy is . . .

Teaching is . . .

Caring is . . .

Love is . . .

Travelling is . . .

Talking is . . .

Shopping is . . .

Eating is . . .

Goodness is . . .

Television is . . .

Parenting is . . .

Gardening is . . .

Sightseeing is . . .

Working is . . .

Pleasure is . . .

Flying is . . .

How important is thinking for you?

How important is it for you to know your thoughts?

'How do I know what I think until I have said it?'
Does this apply to you?

When do you use thoughts rather than feelings to solve a problem?

Does your head rule your heart or your heart rule your head?

Some people say that men are **thinkers** and women are **feelers**. Do you agree with this statement?

Under what circumstances do you share your thoughts with your family or friends?

What kind of thoughts do you share with others?

What kind of thoughts do you hide?

What thoughts are you proud of?

What thoughts are you afraid of?

What thoughts are you ashamed of?

What do these thoughts do to you as a person?

Feelings

fear

anger

joy

grief

happiness

anguish

anxiety

frustration

love

conflict

hostility

peacefulness

rejection

anticipation

excitement

confusion

annoyance

hate

add anything you like to this list of feelings . . .

As you read down this list, and add any feelings of your own, be aware of any feeling-word(s) which you noticed particularly or which *rang a bell* for you.

Be aware of that word and the feeling which it conveys to you.

What is it about this feeling that makes it important for you?

'This morning I was **afraid** that a certain friend might phone. I am not always at ease with him. Sure enough he did phone! I told him I was busy, but he didn't hear what I was saying. I **felt** not heard. He talked about his week; it seemed trivial. I got **impatient**. I got **annoyed** with myself for not telling him *good-bye*. But we said some good things too and I also felt **concern** for him. I was left **frustrated** because my plans for the morning were disrupted. I am left with a sense of unease because I am not **assertive** with certain people.'

So don't ring —
SEE IF I CARE!

Most feelings arise in relationships with other people.

Make a list of what feelings you associate with what person.

person   **feeling**

. . . .

. . . .

. . . .

. . . .

. . . .

. . . .

. . . .

. . . .

. . . .

. . . .

. . . .

. . . .

. . . .

. . . .

- What does this say about you?

- What does this say about the other person?

- Would you like to change the feeling-relationship with any of these persons? To what would you like to change it?

- Is it better to have a long list or a short list?

- Are there people in your life with whom you have no feeling-relationship?

- Are you mostly aware of your feelings?

- Can you normally name a feeling accurately?

- When you get angry, how does this normally manifest itself?

- When you are happy, how does this normally manifest itself?

- Who or what helps you (or might help you) to know your feelings more accurately?

make a note of anything . . .

In the next few days be aware of your feelings more particularly, and name any feeling as and when you experience it. When you can name something you have a handle to deal with it and use it effectively, rather than be used by it.

(Feelings and how to use them in helping relationships are dealt with in the package *Beginning with Empathy*.)

Working on your feelings from a book is not easy. Feelings are generated by some event and then interiorised. They often only make sense when they are **exteriorised**, again by talking about them. Through this movement of going in and coming out, meaning is discovered: the meaning for a feeling; the meaning of a situation, an event, a relationship.

make a note of anything . . .

Motivation

What keeps you going?

What makes you get up in the morning?

'Motivation consists of external and internal factors. An external weighing up of a situation, making an *estimate* leads to an internal situation of *esteem*. That in turn leads to the response which characterises a person.'

Tschudin, 1990

Motivations tend to be . . .

a wish to perform well

conforming to certain standards *(your own, or other people's)*

better salary

recognition from other people

genuine interest

the need to be needed

exerting control

self-respect

add your own . . .

. . . .

. . . .

. . . .

. . . .

. . . .

. . . .

. . . .

. . . .

. . . .

Which of these motivators apply mostly to you?

Some people say that mistakes and failure are
motivators.

Do you agree   for yourself?
in the case of others?

What are some things in your life which you
cannot change?

What areas can you control?

Are you content with these situations?

People who know their values are more likely to live life positively.

'People who are (or appear to be) flighty, apathetic, moody, rebellious, conforming and submissive, or phoney, may be people who have not come to grips with their own values.'

Tschudin, 1986

Values are held internally but expressed externally. They express what a person is: they convey the **reality** of a person. When a person's values and actions coincide, we speak of an integrated person, a person who can be trusted.

You might like to think where in your life your values and your actions coincide. Where do they not coincide?

Do people say that you are a person of integrity? Do they copy your values?

Be aware of the areas where you feel that integrity is missing. Be aware of it – not for condemnation or guilt, but for possible growth.

In order to discover what, or who, you are, you need to be aware of your values, your guideposts and also your boundaries.

Below are a few value statements, to direct your thinking.
add your own – as many as you like . . .

owning my own house

preserving justice

being private

being in control of my experiences

caring for my parents

able to express myself freely

having a job with a pension

freedom to worship

. . . .

. . . .

. . . .

. . . .

. . . .

. . . .

Now put these statements in order of priority by giving them numbers.

Needs and wants

Our values are based on our needs and wants. Modern advertising often makes it difficult for us to know the difference.

Do you need another coat or do you want one?

Do you need a computer or do you want one?

Do you need another sandwich or do you want it?

Think of 10 things which you have bought in the last week. Did you need them or want them? Put them into either of the two categories.

needs   **wants**

. . . .

. . . .

. . . .

. . . .

. . . .

. . . .

. . . .

. . . .

. . . .

. . . .

What does this table reveal to you? Stay with it for a moment and be as honest with your answer as you can.

Now write down what your basic needs are as you see them. They may be material needs: *clothes, food*; social needs: *clean air, justice*; or emotional/spiritual needs: *close relationships*.

You might like to make a similar list for your partner/friend who is closest to you.

As you compare the two lists, be aware of the differences.
Does this show any difficulties?

Look at the differences, and be aware of any areas which might need attention.

When you look at your wants and needs you might also look at them in relation to strengths and weaknesses.
Is a want a temptation?
What do you need for your professional development?

Perhaps you could stay with these thoughts and make any notes you like. If you need more space or help with this *and other aspect(s)*, you may be able to use the workshop for this. Be aware then if this is a need or a want, a strength or a weakness.

Supernatural experiences

Many people have psychic or spiritual experiences. Lewis (1987) states that nurses as a professional group are more likely to have such experiences than the general population. He claims that 67% of nurses are aware of premonitions, the presence of spiritual beings, have seen people after they had died, experienced healing, and had prayers answered.

'When working in intensive care, they came to tissue-type a boy for a kidney transplant, as they were expecting him to die, though the test for brain death wasn't going to be done until the next day. I said "How dare you!" and told them he was going to be OK. I nursed him all night but when I told the sister the next morning that I thought his consciousness level was lighter and he would wake up, she poured scorn on me and they all laughed. Twelve hours later I got a phone call at home to say he was sitting up in bed, demanding food.'

Lewis, 1987

- Have you had any experience of a world or powers beyond the normal?

- Do you know of someone who has?

- What do you think such experiences tell you and those who have them?

- If you think that they are important, why do you think this is so?

- Why do you think that nurses are more prone to have such experiences than the general population?

- What would you say is the difference between psychic and spiritual experiences?

- To what extent do they help in any awareness?

- To what extent do such experiences help in personal development?

make a note about any of these questions you feel will be helpful to you . . .

Religion was one of the topics which used not to be discussed in certain circles.

It is claimed that religion is a private affair. You might like to think how religion – or Christianity – influences life in this country.

As a nurse you will have many people with a strong faith, no faith, some faith. You will have met many different faiths and practices.

Try to call to mind an incident of an expression of faith by someone which you liked or respected or influenced you positively.

Can you remember why this was so?

Remember an incident which you did not like or agree with.

Remember if you can, why this was so and what your reaction was.

Do you have a personal religion or faith? What is the essence of that faith?

Write your own personal creed . . .

now

10 years ago

10 years from now

On the scale below mark where you would place the importance of faith or religion

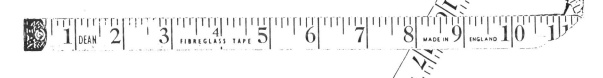

What has changed in your attitude between 10 years ago and now?

What is the essence of that change?

What do you think may be an influencing factor in the future?

- People do not need a religion to be good.

- Religion is practical – mystics are out of touch.

- All religions are basically the same.

- **'Religion is the opium of the people.'** *Marx*

- Prayer is the highest form of care for others.

Think about these statements, and be aware what they say to you.

you might like to make your own statements . . .

I wish people would stop saying I don't exist – it makes me feel so insecure . . .

Intuition is being aware of a greater whole, a wholeness of purpose, of ideas, of events.

Some people do not trust intuition because there is nothing logical about it. That is precisely its strength.

When we are with other people we have '*hunches*'; we use a '*sixth sense*'. Where there is a relationship there are also unexplainable '*vibes*' which we are aware of, and use, but often do not name.

We can only learn to be aware of intuitions by listening, to ourselves, the other person, and the relationship.

When have you used intuition, and how?

Is there a pattern to your intuitions?

'We can increase our intuitive capacity if we will
acknowledge the possibility of our receiving
intuitions, recognise their value, cherish them
when they come, and finally, learn to *trust* them.'

Ferrucci, 1982

The unconscious or unknown

Our unknown and unconscious aspects are part of ourselves and our personalities. These aspects reveal themselves at strategic or important times in our lives, such as . . .

in dreams

in times of crises

through illness

through suffering

through bereavement

through changing relationships, such as marriage, the birth of a child, separation.

Other people often know us better than we know ourselves. We know others better than they know themselves.

Think back to an experience when someone told you a **home truth**. What did that make you feel?

Illness or hospitalization is often **a moment of truth**: we become aware of an aspect of ourselves which we had neglected or not known about.
What have been your **moments of truth**? What did you learn from them?

'If you can dream – and not make
dreams your master . . .'

Kipling

'Dreams are part of human
evolution, and whether the individual notices it or not, dreams will
always be contributing to his
efforts to fulfil the whole of his
potential, concentrating especially
on those parts that he is
neglecting and that are therefore
threatening the growth and
development of his personality.'

Chetwynd, 1972

Remembering dreams is one way of bringing the
unconscious or unknown to the surface. In doing so,
we allow these aspects to become part of ourselves
as persons of wholeness and integrity.

As part of learning awareness and becoming aware, you might keep a dream diary. At the end of each week read through the entries and try to detect patterns or similarities.
Continue some dreams after they are finished.

If you were walking in a house, now in your awake imagination walk on further, and continue your dream in this way.
If there were people, in imagination become these people and continue the dream.
In imagination become any objects which were present in the dream and feel as they might feel now.

Dreams are full of symbols of every kind. Every gesture can be interpreted in symbols. Whatever the symbol means to you spontaneously is probably right.

Many of the symbols point to the integration of body, mind and spirit, or indeed reveal the splits present between them.

All symbols are powerful if and when we allow ourselves to take them seriously and use them for a better understanding of ourselves.

Are there any symbols which you particularly recognise or feel are yours?

as part of these exercises of awareness you could draw your particular symbol(s) here . . .

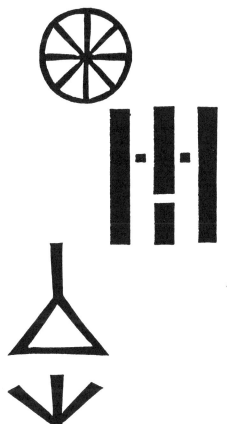

Symbols, patterns, memories, fantasies – these are all important aspects of the inner world. Here they **rule OK**. They give shape to who and what we are. Becoming aware of them can be an exciting discovery. But it can also be a painful exercise.

This discovery, this self-awareness, is not for its own sake. It is for more and better functioning as a person. The symbols, day-dreams and night-dreams are there for us to use them. They help us to discover meaning for ourselves and others.

'Let there be no scales to weigh
your unknown treasure; And seek
not the depths of your knowledge
with staff or sounding line.
For self is a sea
boundless and measureless.'

Gibran, 1926

Meaning

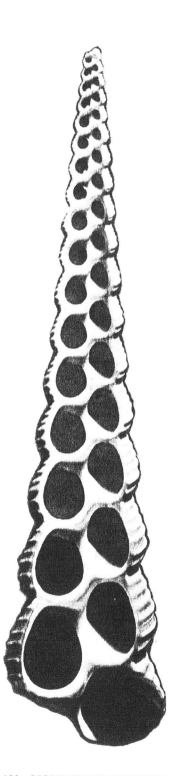

'The serious problems of life are never fully solved . . . The meaning and design of a problem seem not to lie in its solution, but in our working at it incessantly.'

Jung, 1933

'Life does not mean something vague, but something very real and concrete, just as life's tasks are also very real and concrete. They form a man's destiny, which is different and unique for each individual.'

Frankl, 1962

The inner world of a person is often chaotic. Contradictions, skeletons in cupboards, wild and untamed animals, passions of love and hate, symbols and archetypes which make no sense, stores of power, energy and creativity – all these, and many more, are present and present themselves at different times. They are the raw materials of the personality. It is up to us to use them.

The integrity of the personality depends on how we use all the parts of ourselves.
As a garden, which is not tended, quickly disintegrates and becomes a wilderness, so the inner life, when it is not attended to, deteriorates into chaos. But as in a wilderness, there is an almost ferocious will to survive, so in the inner chaos, the will to survival is stronger than the force of destruction. Finding meaning is finding that will, co-operating with it and using it.

'We find the meaning
of a situation or event
by doing a deed
by experiencing a value
by suffering.'

Frankl, 1962

As much as possible, look back over your life and
remember the events which formed you:

e.g.   an accident

the death of someone

passing an exam

make a note of them and list as many as you can . . .

. . . .

. . . .

. . . .

. . . .

. . . .

. . . .

. . . .

. . . .

. . . .

From this list pick out the three most significant

. . . .

. . . .

. . . .

Think about each event, and note what was special about it for you and in which way it marked you.

Was it an event in which you achieved or accomplished something?

Did you experience a particular value, ie something which you hold as important, such as the love of a person, the way you care, a principle you stand by?

Did you discover something about yourself through suffering?
Was it your own or someone else's suffering?
Not only Mother Teresa has found meaning by going to the slums of Calcutta . . .

Be aware of these events, and be aware of how they have shaped you. You may not only like what they have done to you. We gain from them not by fighting them, but by using – integrating – them.

It is possible that a pattern emerges for you. If it doesn't, don't worry: calling such events to the awareness is work which may take a long time. Simply be aware of what is happening for you. In the workshop and in groups you may have the possibility to discover more about yourself and others which may be of help.

Self-awareness leads to discovering meaning in your life, in your work and in events around you. **Self-awareness** gives you a direction, a sense of purpose. You become a person of integrity.

'As a person understands and prizes self, the self becomes more congruent with the experiencings. The person thus becomes more real, more genuine. These tendencies . . . enable the person to be a more effective growth-enhancer for himself or herself. There is a greater freedom to be the true, whole person.'

Rogers, 1980

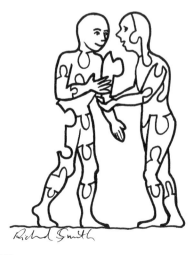

- Integrity is about knowing your strengths and needs correctly and not pretending about them.

- Integrity is knowing what choices there are.

- Integrity is knowing what you can change and knowing what you cannot change.

- Integrity is using your gifts and strengths adequately and not hiding them.

- Integrity is knowing your boundaries and going as far as your boundaries, and not being afraid of over-stepping them at the right moment.

- Integrity is being different, unique, exceptional – and accepting that everybody else is different, unique and exceptional.

- Integrity is crying with those who cry, and laughing with those who laugh.

Look back over the exercises and over the learning which you have done.
What stands out mostly for you as a learning experience?

Do you feel that you have *absorbed* this learning already?

In what way are you now more aware of yourself?

Where do you see that you have developed as a person, and as a nurse?

'*Why be moral? Why be caring?*
has to do with who I am,
with ends or ultimate purposes.
Perhaps this kind of question is
beyond ethical reasoning because
its answer is already given. It is
not to be determined but to be
discovered.'

Roach, 1984

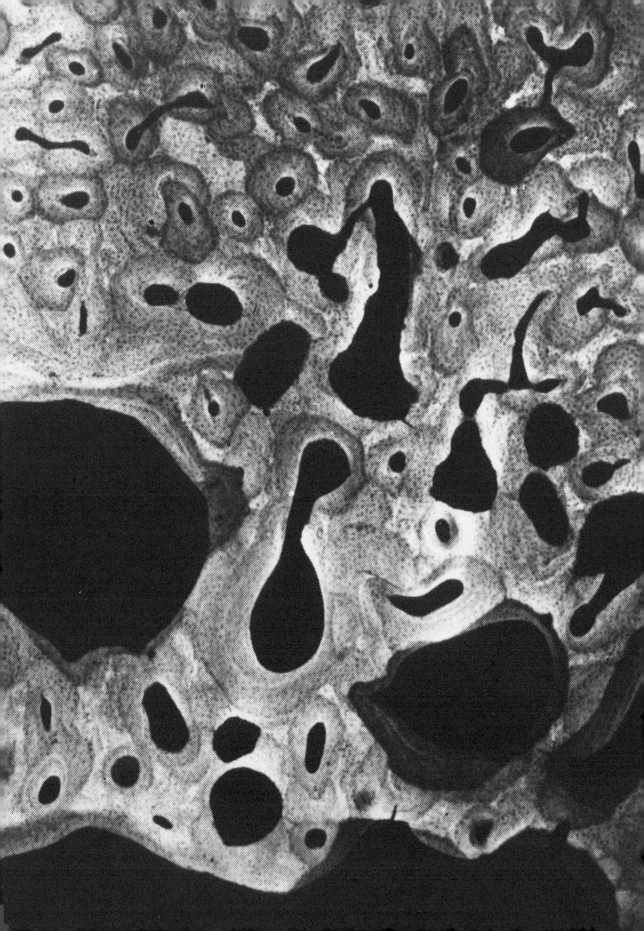

◁ *This is a microradiograph of a normal femoral shaft.*
In the context of this book try to look at this picture as something you relate to; something beautiful; something artistic. What does it say to you?

As one example, let us take the microscope which can reveal through histological slides either a world of per se beauty or else a world of threat, danger and pathology. A section of cancer seen through a microscope, if only we can forget that it is cancer, can be seen as a beautiful and intricate and awe-inspiring organisation. A mosquito is a wondrous object if seen as an end-in-itself. Viruses under the electron microscope are fascinating objects (or, at least, they *can* be if we can only forget their human relevance).

Maslow, 1968

*   *   *   *   *   *   *

Awareness is not a one-off event. It is an ongoing process, a journey. One of the most effective ways of being aware that I know of is looking back over the day and being thankful for people I met, events that took place, things that were given and received. *Counting blessings* is a way of putting much of life into perspective.

I hope that you find your own way of learning awareness, and that you may have much satisfaction through it.

May you have every success in your work.

References and further reading
Titles with an asterisk * are suggested for further reading

B

Bible, Jerusalem Bible version 1966, London, Darton Longman & Todd

Bono, De E. 1967, *The five-day course in thinking*. New York. Basic Books.

* **Bond, M.** 1986, *Stress and self-awareness: a guide for nurses.* London, Heinemann.

Buber, M. 1937, *I and thou.* Translation (1970) Kaufmann. Edinburgh, T. & T. Clark.

* **Burnard, P.** 1985, *Learning human skills.* London, Heinemann.

C

* **Chetwynd, T.** 1972, *Dictionary for dreamers.* London, Paladin.

* **Chetwynd, T.** 1982, *A dictionary of symbols.* London, Granada.

* **Clark, C. C.** 1978, *Assertive skills for nurses.* Rockville, Maryland, Aspen.

D

* **Dickson, A.** 1985, *The mirror within – a new look at sexuality.* London, Quartet.

E

Egan, G. 1986, *The skilled helper*, 3rd edn. Belmont, CA. Wadsworth Publishing Co.

F

* **Ferrucci, P.** 1982, *What we may be.* Wellingborough, Turnstone Press.

* **Frankl, V.** 1962, *Man's search for meaning.* New York, Pocket Books.

G

Gibran, K. 1926, *The prophet.* London, Heinemann.

J

* **Jourard, S.** 1971, *The transparent self.* New York, Van Nostrand Reinhold.

Jung, C. 1933, *Modern man in search of a soul.* London, Routledge & Kegan Paul.

L

Lewis, D. 1987, *All in good faith.* NURSING TIMES 83(11), p40–43.

M **Maslow, A.** 1968, *Toward a psychology of being*. New York, Van Nostrand Reinhold, p76.

* **Mayeroff, M.** 1972, *On caring*. New York, Harper & Row.

N **Nouwen, H., McNeill, D., Morrison, D.** 1982, *Compassion*. London, Darton, Longman & Todd.

P * **Pearce, J.** 1981, *The bond of power: meditation and wholeness*. London, Routledge & Kegan Paul.

R * **Roach, M. S.** 1984, *Caring: the human mode of being, implications for nursing*. University of Toronto.

* **Rogers, C. R.** 1961, *On becoming a person*. London, Constable.

Rogers, C. R. 1980, *A way of being*. Boston, Houghton Mifflin.

S * **Simonton, O. C. & Matthews-Simonton, S. & Creighton, J.** 1978, *Getting well again*. New York, Bantam Books.

* **Stevens, O.** 1971, *Awareness: exploring, experimenting, experiencing*. Moab, Utah, Real People Press.

T * **Tschudin, V.** 1986, *Ethics in nursing: the caring relationship*. London, Heinemann.

* **Tschudin, V.** 1990, *Managing yourself*. London, Macmillan.

W * **Wilson, M.** 1986, *Group theory/process for nursing practice*. Hemel Hempstead, Prentice/Hall International.